VOLUME 11 ~ LATE INTERMEDIATE TO EARLY ADVANCED

MODERN *Masterworks*

10 Captivating Works for Piano by Ravel, Bortkievich, Martinů, Poulenc and others

AF731887

This book is dedicated to Richard Magrath

Cover art: Electric Prisms, 1914
by Sonia Delaunay (French, 1885–1979)

Alfred

Compiled and edited by JANE MAGRATH

Preface

Performing contemporary literature can be one of the most rewarding musical experiences for pianists. The music in this two-volume set was chosen for its vitality and variety of sounds and styles, from impressionism to polytonal writing and dissonant harmonies. Some standard literature not often heard in performance was included to provide performers with adventures into new musical directions. Students will be exhilarated and enchanted with the vibrant rhythms and sonorities as well as the captivating sounds of these selections. Every effort has been made to remain faithful to the composer's original indications in the score, though some fingerings and occasional re-distributions of passagework have been added. A possible order for repertoire study has been suggested in each book to guide students through a range of difficulty levels.

Warm thanks and sincere appreciation to Morty and Iris Manus and E.L. Lancaster for their support and help with these volumes.

A Special Note to the Performer

These pieces have been selected with you, the performer, in mind. Every attempt has been made to provide music of the highest quality that will be appealing to you and your audiences. Best wishes for many hours of delight, joy and beauty as you practice and perform these selections. Most importantly, listen carefully to your playing as you practice, and enjoy every piece that you read or study!

Jane Magrath

Suggested Progressive Order for Study

Bartók, Béla	Folk Dance
Bortkievich, Sergei	The Sleigh Drive, Op. 21, No. 2
Debussy, Claude	Album Leaf
Martinů, Bohuslav	Columbine Dances
Martinů, Bohuslav	Columbine Sings
Martinů, Bohuslav	A Game of Tag
Martinů, Bohuslav	Puppet Show
Ravel, Maurice	Prélude
Debussy, Claude	La fille aux cheveux de lin
Poulenc, Francis	Valse

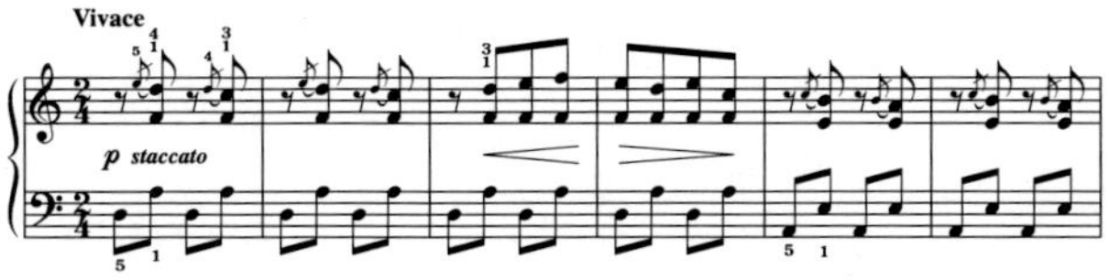
Vivace
p staccato

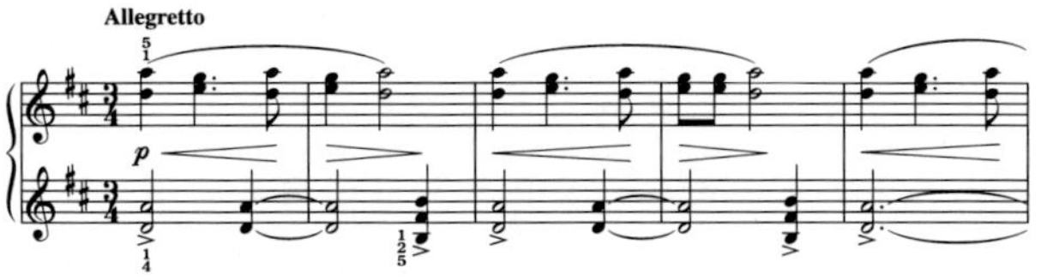
Allegretto
p

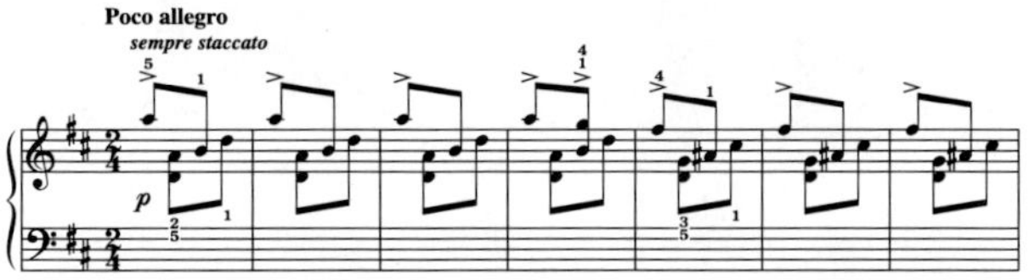
Poco allegro
sempre staccato
p

Lento
cantabile
p
con pedale

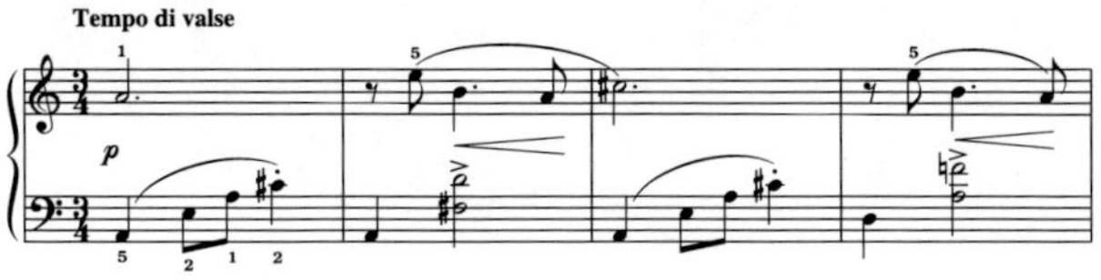
Tempo di valse
p

Assez vif ⓐ
mf
f

Assez lent et très expressif (d'un rythme libre) ⓐ
p

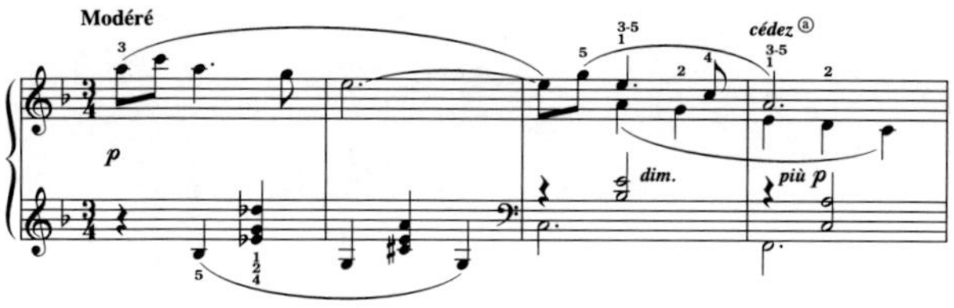
Modéré
cédez ⓐ
p
dim.
più p

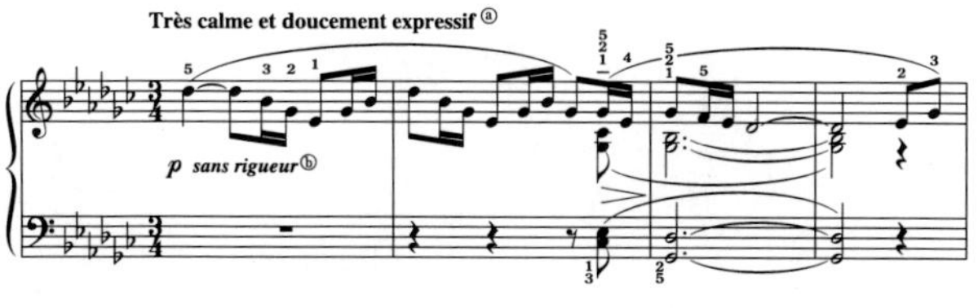
Très calme et doucement expressif ⓐ
p sans rigueur ⓑ

Allegro
f
p
cresc.

LITERATURE LEVELS
for Modern Masterworks, Volumes I & II

based on
The Pianist's Guide to Standard Teaching and Performance Literature
by Jane Magrath

Book covers are placed to show approximate grading of each volume based on the Level chart from *The Pianist's Guide to Standard Teaching and Performance Literature.*

Level 1	Bartók *Mikrokosmos, Volume 1*
Level 2	Türk *Pieces for Beginners*
Level 3	Latour *Sonatinas*
	Kabalevsky *Pieces for Young People, Op. 39*
Level 4	*Anna Magdalena Bach Notebook*
	Gurlitt *Album for the Young, Op. 140*
	Tchaikovsky *Album for the Young, Op. 39*
Level 5	*Anna Magdalena Bach Notebook*
	Attwood, Lynes *Sonatinas*
	Menotti *Poemetti*
Level 6	Clementi *Sonatinas, Op. 36*
	Burgmüller *25 Progressive Pieces, Op. 100*
Level 7	Kuhlau and moderate Diabelli *Sonatinas*
	Bach easiest *Two-Part Inventions*
	Bach *Short Preludes*
	Dello Joio *Lyric Pieces for the Young*
Level 8	Bach moderately difficult *Two-Part Inventions*
	Beethoven easiest variation sets
	Field *Nocturnes*
	Schumann *Album Leaves, Op. 124*
	Schubert *Waltzes*
	Turina *Miniatures*
Level 9	Bach *Two-Part Inventions*
	Haydn easiest sonata movements
	Mendelssohn easiest *Songs Without Words*
	Chopin easiest *Mazurkas*
Level 10	Bach easiest *Three-Part Inventions*
	Chopin easiest *Nocturnes*
	Beethoven *Sonatas, Op. 49, 79*
	Mozart *Sonata, K. 283*
	Muczynski *Preludes*

Volume I

Volume II

The Sleigh Drive

Sergei Bortkievich (1877–1952)
Op. 21, No. 2

Vivace

31
marcato
38
45
52
poco cresc.
59

66
73
più f
80
sf
87
ff
94
rit.
fff

Puppet Show

Valse

Bohuslav Martinů
(1890–1959)

26
Tempo di valse
mf espressivo
31
37
43
rit.
a tempo
p
49
poco f

54
8va
cresc.
f
59
rit.
mf
p
63
pp
rit. poco a poco
Allegretto
68
p
73
poco f
p

78
mf
83
p
cresc.
Allegro vivo
8va
88
sf
f
93
mf
p
98
Meno
poco mf
Poco andante
p

A Game of Tag

Bohuslav Martinů
(1890–1959)

Poco allegro
sempre staccato

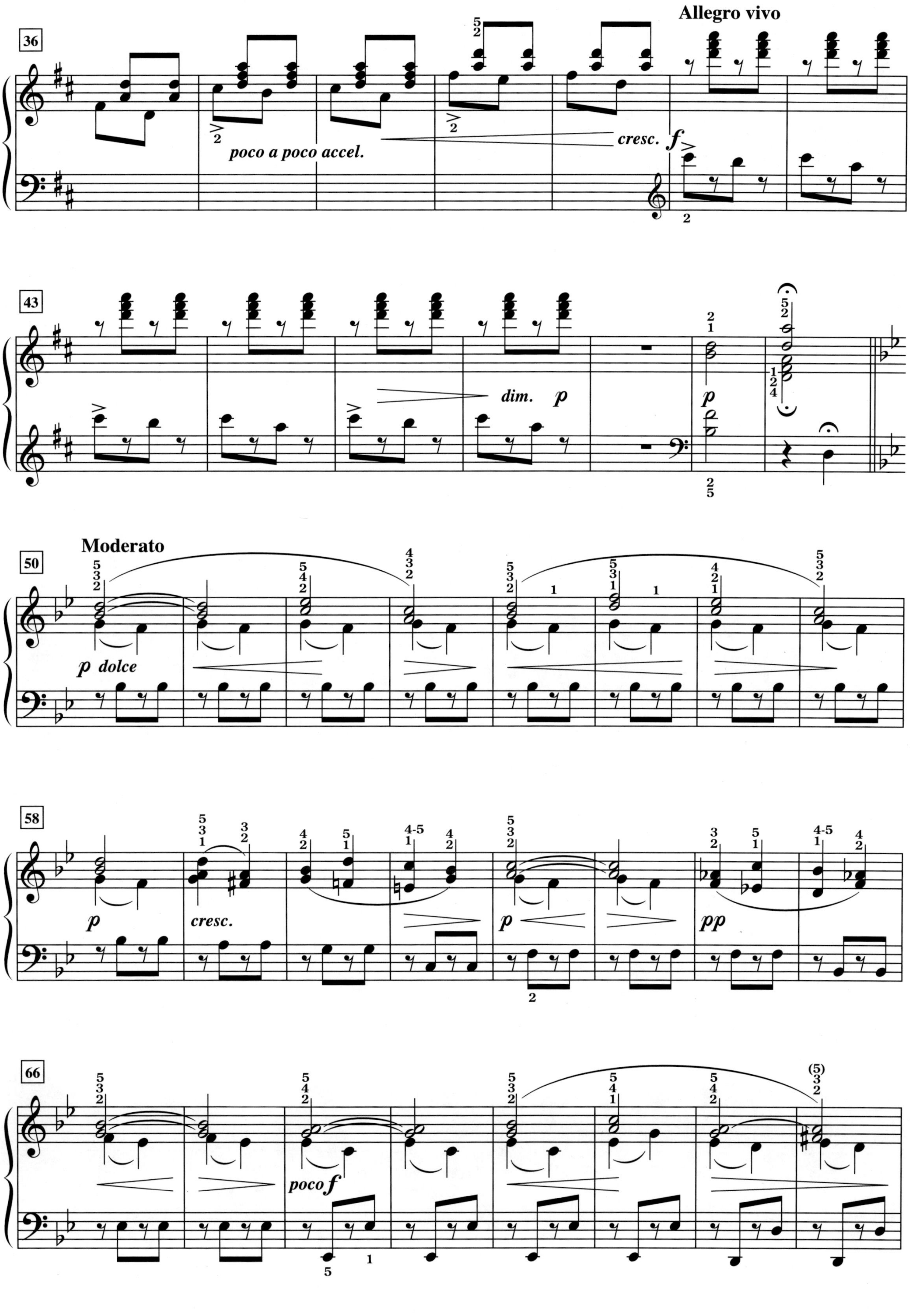
Allegro vivo
36
poco a poco accel.
cresc.
f
43
dim.
p
Moderato
50
p dolce
58
p
cresc.
pp
66
poco f

74
a tempo
f
rit.
mf
82
90
sostenuto
p
pp
Tempo I (Poco allegro)
98
105
mf
poco accel.
f
dim. e rit.

112
a tempo
119
126
133
Allegro vivo
poco a poco accel.
cresc.
140
dim.

Columbine Sings

Bohuslav Martinů
(1890–1959)

26
ff
sfz
pp
31
36
diminuendo
Fine
pp
Scherzando
42
p
50
p

58
p
65
72
mf
mf
77
f
8va
f
LH 2
D. C. al Fine
82
RH 3
mf dim. e rit.
p
pp

Columbine Dances

Valse

Bohuslav Martinů
(1890–1959)

Tempo di valse

Poco vivo
poco rit.
meno f
a tempo
rit.

43
Tempo I
47
52
57
1.
61
2.
8va
m.d.

Valse

Francis Poulenc
(1899–1963)

ⓐ Rather fast. Composer's metronome mark is ♩. = 96.

ⓑ Forcefully strike the appogiaturas.

ⓒ In a very singing manner.

ⓓ With urgency ⓔ Supple ⓕ Without pedal

ⓖ With charm ⓗ Play the low A as a grace note before the beat.

ⓘ Dry ⓙ Well phrased (legato) ⓚ Brilliant

Prélude

Maurice Ravel
(1875–1937)

Assez lent et très expressif (d'un rythme libre)ⓐ

ⓐ Rather slow and very expressive (rhythmically free)

ⓑ The composer left a pedal marking here, indicating the use of pedal in this piece. The pedal in meas. 20–22 is also the composer's.

13
ralenti
13
ralenti
au mouvt
16
20
ralenti
24
Très lent
pp

Album Leaf

Claude Debussy
(1862–1918)

ⓐ Hold back ⓑ A tempo ⓒ Press forward ⓓ Slowing down

ⓔ A little more lively

La fille aux cheveux de lin

(The Girl with the Flaxen Hair)

Claude Debussy
(1862–1918)

Key: e♭ minor

Très calme et doucement expressif ⓐ

ⓐ Very calm and gently expressive
ⓑ Without strictness; freely
ⓒ Play LH low E♭ and B♭ together on the beat, quickly followed by the G and B♭.

ⓓ Without heaviness ⓔ Very gentle ⓕ Whispered and slowing little by little

Folk Dance

Béla Bartók
(1881–1945)